21st Century Junior Library

Iguanodon

by Lucia Raatma

CHERRY LAKE PUBLISHING * ANN ARBOR, MICHIGAN

Published in the United States of America by Cherry Lake Publishing
Ann Arbor, Michigan
www.cherrylakepublishing.com

Content Adviser: Gregory M. Erickson, PhD, Dinosaur Paleontologist, Department of Biological
Science, Florida State University, Tallahassee, Florida

Reading Adviser: Marla Conn, Read with Me Now

Photo Credits: Cover and page 14, ©North Wind Picture Archives/Alamy; pages 4, 12, and 18,
©dieKleinert/Alamy; page 6, ©Florilegius/Alamy; page 8, ©Universal Images Group Limited/Alamy;
page 10, ©TomBham/Alamy; page 16, ©vario images GmbH & Co.KG/Alamy; page 20, ©Dylan
Garcia Travel Images/Alamy

LIBRARY OF CONGRESS CATALOGING-IN-PUBLICATION DATA
Raatma, Lucia.
  Iguanodon/by Lucia Raatma.
    p. cm.—(21st century junior library. dinosaurs)
  Includes bibliographical references and index.
  ISBN 978-1-61080-464-6 (lib. bdg.)—ISBN 978-1-61080-551-3 (e-book)—
ISBN 978-1-61080-638-1 (pbk.)
  1. Iguanodon—Juvenile literature. I. Title.
  QE862.O65R329 2013
  567.914—dc23   2012003504

*Cherry Lake Publishing would like to acknowledge the work of
The Partnership for 21st Century Skills.
Please visit* www.21stcenturyskills.org *for more information.*

Printed in the United States of America
Corporate Graphics Inc.
July 2012
CLFA11

CONTENTS

The last *Iguanodons* died out millions
of years ago.

What Was an Iguanodon?

Imagine a dinosaur that could run on its back legs. And it could walk on all four legs. That is the *Iguanodon*. It lived about 125 million years ago. It was one of the first types of dinosaurs ever discovered. Today, all dinosaurs are **extinct**.

The *Iguanodon* was the second kind of dinosaur ever found.

The name *Iguanodon* means "**iguana tooth**." The scientist who first discovered it gave it this name. He thought the dinosaur's teeth looked like those of an iguana. This first discovery was made in England. But *Iguanodons* lived all over the world. They have been found in Belgium, the United States, Germany, and North Africa.

Look!

Find a picture of an iguana. You might look in a book or online. Study its mouth. Do you think it looks like an *Iguanodon*?

The *Iguanodon* walked with its tail
lifted off the ground.

What Did an *Iguanodon* Look Like?

The main part of an *Iguanodon*'s body was large and bulky. It had a tail that was thick and stiff. Each back foot had three toes. Its front feet had five. Its back legs were much longer than its front ones. In fact, its front legs looked more like arms.

The *Iguanodon*'s teeth were all hidden along the insides of its cheeks.

One special thing about the *Iguanodon* was its mouth. It looked something like a bird's beak. However, the *Iguanodon* had no teeth in the front of its mouth. Instead, all of its teeth lined the inside of its cheeks.

Scientists first thought the *Iguanodon*'s large spikes belonged on the dinosaur's nose.

Another important feature of the *Iguanodon* was its front feet. Each one had a **spike**. These spikes were very big. In fact, some scientists first thought they were horns. The sharp spikes probably helped the *Iguanodon* fight off **predators**.

Think!

Look at the pictures in this book. Find the *Iguanodon's* spikes. Why do you think scientists first thought they were horns?

An *Iguanodon* stood about three times
as tall as most adult people.

The *Iguanodon* was about 30 feet (9 meters) long. Its hips were about 9 feet (2.7 m) high. But it could stand as tall as 16 feet (5 m). This dinosaur weighed between 4 and 5 tons. That's about the same weight as an African elephant!

Create!

You will need five adults to help you with this. Go outside and ask them to lie on the ground. They should lie end to end. The whole group should be about 25 to 30 feet (7.6 to 9 m) long. Can you imagine a dinosaur that was this long?

Iguanodons often ate plants that grew near rivers, streams, or other water.

How Did an *Iguanodon* Live?

The *Iguanodon* was an **herbivore**. It ate twigs, bushes, ferns, and plant leaves. It could stand up on its back legs. This allowed it to reach high branches. The dinosaur broke off food with its beak. Then it chewed with the teeth along its cheeks.

Living in a herd might have helped protect
hurt or sick *Iguanodons*.

Iguanodons lived in a **herd**. This group helped provide protection from other animals. One *Iguanodon* could stand watch while others slept.

The *Iguanodon* could walk along on all fours. Or it could run on its back legs if it was in danger. It could run as fast as 15 miles (24 kilometers) per hour.

Ask Questions!

Talk to your family and friends. Do they like being a part of a group, like a herd? What are the good parts about living in a group? When do they like to be alone?

Several *Iguanodon* fossils have been found in England.

Scientists first discovered *Iguanodon* remains in the 1800s. They have learned about this dinosaur by studying its **fossils**. One place to see them is at the Royal Belgian Institute of Natural Sciences. This museum is in Brussels, Belgium. Would you like to go fossil hunting one day?

Make a Guess!

Think about dinosaur movies and TV shows you have seen. How many of them featured an *Iguanodon*?

GLOSSARY

extinct (ek-STINGKT) describing a type of plant or animal that has completely died out

fossils (FAH-suhlz) the preserved remains of living things from thousands or millions of years ago

herbivore (HUR-buh-vor) an animal that eats plants rather than other animals

herd (HURD) a large group of animals

iguana (i-GWAN-uh) a large tropical lizard

predators (PRED-uh-turz) animals that live by hunting other animals for food

spike (SPIKE) a large, sharp, pointed object

FIND OUT MORE

BOOKS

Gray, Susan Heinrichs. *Iguanodon*. Mankato, MN: The Child's World, 2010.

Rockwood, Leigh. *Iguanodon*. New York: PowerKids Press, 2012.

WEB SITES

Discovery: Dinosaur Central
http://dsc.discovery.com/dinosaurs/ iguanodon.html
Learn about the unique features of the *Iguanodon*.

Royal Belgian Institute of Natural Sciences— Dinosaurs
www.naturalsciences.be/museum/ dinosaurs
Check out this site to learn more about Europe's largest dinosaur collection.

INDEX

ABOUT THE AUTHOR

Lucia Raatma has written dozens of books for young readers. She and her family live in the Tampa Bay area of Florida. They enjoy looking at the dinosaur fossils at the local science museum.